LEADING

like a

LION

DAVID WEBB

WESTBOW
PRESS®

A DIVISION OF THOMAS NELSON
& ZONDERVAN

All Scripture quotations are taken from the King James Bible.

WestBow Press books may be ordered through booksellers or by contacting:

WestBow Press
A Division of Thomas Nelson & Zondervan
1663 Liberty Drive
Bloomington, IN 47403
www.westbowpress.com
1 (866) 928-1240

ISBN: 978-1-9736-5343-1 (hc)
ISBN: 978-1-9736-5341-7 (hc)
ISBN: 978-1-9736-5342-4 (e)

Library of Congress Control Number: 2019902041

Printed in the United States.

WestBow Press rev. date: 04/02/2019

This book is dedicated to the love of my life, my wife, Genell, whose sweet encouragement has inspired me over and over to follow my dreams. She is worth far more than rubies.

Contents

Chapter 1

LEADING LIKE A LION

And one of the elders saith unto me, Weep not: behold, the Lion of the tribe of Judah, the Root of David, hath prevailed.

—Revelation 5:5 (KJV)

Alexander the Great said, "An army of sheep, led by a lion, is better than an army of lions led by a sheep."

When the leader's mind is weak, opposition is a problem. When the leader's mind is simply balanced, the opposition is challenging. When the leader's mind is strong, the opposition becomes an opportunity. Just knowing what is right is not good enough; we must do what is right. Lead like a lion.

Napoleon Bonaparte said, "If you build an army of one hundred lions and their leader is a dog, in any fight, the lions will die like a dog. But if you build an army of one hundred dogs and their leader is a lion, all dogs will fight as a lion."

Author and motivational speaker Jim Rohn said, "The challenge of leadership is to be strong, but not rude; be kind, but not weak; be bold, but not bully; be thoughtful, but not lazy; be humble, but not timid; be proud, but not arrogant; have humor, but without folly."

Let us consider three characteristics of a lion.

1. The Lion Is Not Intimidated

"The wicked flee when no man pursueth: but the righteous are bold as a lion" (Proverbs 28:1 KJV).

There is a spirit of intimidation roaming free in our land. Bullies roam the playgrounds of our public schools; activist judges are no longer interpreting the law but choosing to impose their own agendas on the citizens of this great nation. I am ashamed to say that these tactics are no longer confined to the public arena but have made their way into the church. In some cases, members with money or prominent parishioners are bent on imposing their will upon the church of the living God. Few will stand up to the intimidator for fear of losing tithe or perhaps membership moving on to a hireling's church. *We must lead like lions!* We must not back down. A lion does not bow to the opinion of a mouse. Journalist Herbert Swope said, "I can't give you a sure-fire formula for success, but I can give you a formula for failure: try to please everybody all the time."

2. The Lion Is Not an Isolationist

"The wolf also shall dwell with the lamb, and the leopard shall lie down with the kid; and the calf and the young lion and the fatling together" (Isaiah 11:6–9 KJV).

Lions are the only cat that forms social groups. Could it be that in our attempt to retain personal purity, we isolate ourselves out of fear of being contaminated? We should be insulated, but not isolated. How can we be salt and light, as Christ commanded, if we are confined inside our four walls? The condition called isolation can become so acute that we can disfellowship everyone until we are the only fellow in our ship! How sad.

Abraham Lincoln said, "Believing everyone is dangerous, but believing nobody is more dangerous." We must not mix and mingle with the world. Doctrinal issues cannot be compromised. However, when we separate over preferences, we are practicing the first page in the devil's playbook. We need one another.

At the Richland Holiness Camp Meeting in the 1980s, Bro. Ralph Cox said that the Swiss had developed a device that would split the human hair 250 different ways. He said it reminded him of some church people.

In the late 1800s, there were two deacons in a small Baptist church in Mayfield, Kentucky. They didn't get along and opposed each other in any decision relating to the church. One particular Sunday, a deacon put up a small wooden peg on the back wall so the minister could hang up his hat. When the other deacon discovered the peg, he was outraged that he had not been consulted. Parishioners in the church took sides, and eventually there was a split congregation. To this day, they say you can find, in Mayfield, Kentucky, the Anti-Peg Baptist Church.

Lincoln said, "Nearly all men can stand adversity, but if you want to test a man's character, give him power." Lead like a lion!

3. The Lion Is Not Inferior

"A lion which is strongest among beasts, and turneth not away for any" (Proverbs 30:30 KJV)

Eleanor Roosevelt said, "No one can make you feel inferior without your consent." How many businesses, churches, and homes suffer because of inferiority? Let us come to grips that there will always be someone better than us. How much better we would be to enjoy the talents and abilities of others and count them as a blessing to our life. On the contrary, one can find reason to exclude them from our lives because we cannot stand that they are better than us.

Secure people are happy for others' success. They encourage the vision, stoke the fire, and offer advice they have learned from the school of hard knocks while reaching for greater things. Author Orrin Woodward said, "Average leaders raise the bar on themselves; good leaders raise the bar for others; great leaders inspire others to raise their own bar."

As leaders, we cannot afford to be afraid to ask for help. Jeffery Benjamin said, "A sign of strength is seen in one who asks for help." Great leaders surround themselves with people who are better than themselves. Many leaders suffer from atelophobia, which is the fear of not being good enough. I feel there are many congregations suffering for lack of staff. Consider the cycle; the local church takes an upswing, attendance increases, and finances are more readily available, but there is a leader at the top who will not relinquish any authority to an assistant/ youth pastor/lay leader. Senior pastors may be fearful, knowing that the help they bring could gain favor and split the church. Therefore, many times unintentionally, a leader slams the lid on the growth, and by default the church begins to decline. My personal experience has been that when the time comes to secure a second man, he should be talented enough to split the church but loyal enough not to. Do not be intimidated. Lead like a lion!

"They shall walk after the Lord: he shall roar like a lion: when he shall roar, then the children shall tremble" (Hosea 11:10 KJV).

Chapter 2

VISIONARIES

Throughout the centuries there were men who took first steps, down new roads, armed with nothing but their own vision.

—Ayn Rand, *Atlas Shrugged*

"By faith Abraham, when he was called to go out into a place which he should after receive for an inheritance, obeyed; and he went out, not knowing whither he went. By faith he sojourned in the land of promise, as in a strange country, dwelling in tabernacles with Isaac and Jacob, the heirs with him of the same promise. For he looked for a city which hath foundations, whose builder and maker is God" (Hebrews 11:8–10 KJV).

More than three hundred years before the time of Christ, Alexander the Great marched across Asia Minor. He led the greatest army ever assembled at that time. They had conquered every foe. No one could stand against them. After reaching the Himalayas, the advance team came back to Alexander full of concern and dismay: "We have marched off the map," they said. "We should go back to where we know." And they had literally marched off the known map at that time. Alexander said, "Mediocre armies always stay within the known areas. Truly great armies always march off the map."

If the army of God is to do great things, we must catch the vision of the great things God has for us and then do them!

Fred Smith is a Christian businessman and management consultant. He is a man who takes hold of sick businesses and makes them well again. He said, "I visit thirty to forty churches per year. Most of them are dead, and they are dead because the minister is dead."

Most churches are under-led, not over-led. Sometimes we will find a pastor who is autocratic—all he wants the people to do is to show up, pay up, and shut up. By and large, most leaders are not assertive, nor are they as aggressive as they could be. They take a laissez-faire approach. Laissez-faire comes from the French, meaning "allow them to do it," suggesting the idea of a hands-off approach to leadership.

A great leader can not only receive the vision from God, but also can convey and lead his congregation to accomplish the formerly unseen. Making announcements from the pulpit is not leadership. True leadership consists of three things:

1. Vision: seeing what needs to be done;
2. Strategy: figuring out how to do it; and
3. Motivation: persuading others to buy into the God-given vision.

In the first century BC, much of the world was still unmapped. When a mapmaker got to the edge of what had been explored, he drew monsters and dragons. The story comes down from that time of a Roman officer who was leading his troops on a mission that took them into unmapped territory—dragon territory. He sent a courier back to Rome with a blunt and slightly desperate message, "We have just marched off the map. Please send new orders." In this hour when nobody seem to know what to do, *we need new orders or fresh vision, clear direction, and motivating passion.*

Most organizations began as risk takers, became caretakers, and wound up as undertakers.

About 350 years ago, a shipload of travelers landed on the northeast coast of America. During that first year they established a townsite. The second year they elected a town government. The third year the town government planned to build a road five miles westward into the wilderness. The fourth year the people tried to impeach their town government because they thought it was a waste of public funds to build a road five miles westward into a wilderness. They said, "Who needed to go there anyway?" Here were people who had the vision to see three thousand miles across an ocean and overcome great hardships to get there. But in just a few years they were not able to see even five miles out of town. How soon we forget the vision and become distracted by the cares of the ministry.

We must not settle for the status quo. We must not meddle in mediocrity. We must break the barrier of "little thinking" to do great things for God. Richard Nixon, in his book *Leaders,* wrote, "All really strong leaders I have known have been highly intelligent, highly disciplined, hard workers, supremely self-confident, driven by a dream, driving others. All have looked beyond the horizon."

Theodore Roosevelt, discussing President John Tyler, said, "He has been called a mediocre man; but this is unwarranted flattery. He is a politician of monumental littleness." The difference between monumental littleness and greatness is not talent, charm, or financial resources. *The difference is vision.*

Surround yourself with people who have vision. When you put small men in big positions, they bring decisions down to their size every time. Author D. K. Caldwell said, "Big men think big; little men don't think."

Attempt something great! J. B. Gambrell said, "It is easier to do large things than little things. A great people cannot be rallied to little things. More people, a hundred to one, will join in a bear hunt than will turn out to kill a mouse."

Sometimes we are so afraid to step out on what God said because of what others say. Robert F. Kennedy made famous the quote of George Bernard Shaw by paraphrasing, "You see things as they are and ask, 'Why?' I dream things as they never were and ask, 'Why not?'"

Could it be that our frame of reference can be too small? My uncle, Brian Hacker, had a granddad who lived in Harlan County, Kentucky, all his life. When he was an old man, he made his first trip to the big city of Louisville, Kentucky. Up to this point he had never been across state lines. The city of Louisville borders the state of Indiana. As they were driving this old gentleman through town, they decided to take him out of state for the first time. As they crossed the John F. Kennedy Bridge into Indiana, the old gentleman looked longingly back across the river and said, "Goodbye, ole US of A." His frame of reference was so small; he thought the United States of America was encompassed by the state boundaries of the bluegrass.

On his first voyage, Christopher Columbus sailed through unknown waters to an unknown destination. Before his voyage, Spain's standards carried three words in Latin. The same words were written on the left edge of the maps of that day. Even the Strait of Gibraltar carried the same three words, chiseled into stone. What were the words? "Ne Plus Ultra"—"No More Beyond." While the world was convinced there was nothing more beyond, Columbus was not. His ships returned, and the discovery of a land of wealth and opportunity "beyond" marked the dawn of a new age. The world was forever changed—so much so, the king of Spain changed the motto of the land to read as it does today. One word on the famed monument was torn away by the lion, making it "Plus Ultra"—"More Beyond"!

Not everyone will be happy about your advances. You may take shots from someone full of jealousy. You could be cut down by fellow clergy who call you a compromiser because they are wrestling with their own incompetence. You will be misunderstood by some who are muddled in mediocrity. Those who feel intimidated by advances made will slander the vision, trying to make themselves look better. Try not to take it personally. Do not lower yourself to the mudslinging. Just because a dog may bark at you doesn't mean you lower yourself to barking back. In other words, a real saint of God follows the Lord's voice and disregards the voice of the gainsayers. Vow not to defend yourself, but let God defend you. The vision is greater than verification. The goal is greater than the gossip. The will of God is greater than the whispering. Nobody wants to be criticized. But if you lead, do not expect everyone to love you. Do not expect everyone to agree with you. Do not expect everyone to see it your way. Great leaders have always incited great controversies. They have acquired strong friends and bitter enemies. To be what God wants you to be, you must believe in your cause enough that you are willing to risk failure, criticism, opposition, termination, financial loss, and even your own life if the cause is big enough. As David said in 1 Samuel 17:29, "Is there not a cause?" (KJV) Thomas Jefferson said, "The man who leads the orchestra must turn his back on the crowd."

What is your vision? Do you know what to do? Do you have clear direction, or are you happily holding your own? In the fairy tale *Alice in Wonderland*, the Cheshire cat said, "If you don't know where you're going, any road will get you there." We cannot afford to be wandering aimlessly without goals and purpose.

Michelangelo said, "The greatest danger for most of us is not that our aim is too high and we miss it but that it is too low and we reach it."

A godly vision is right for the times, right for the church, and right for the people. A godly vision promotes faith rather than fear. A godly vision motivates people to action. A godly vision requires risk taking. A godly vision glorifies God, not people. Vision always entails progress; it is never satisfied with the status quo. William Cary lived by the motto: "Expect great things from God; attempt great things for God."

Joel A. Barker said, "Vision without action is merely a dream. Action without vision just passes the time. Vision with action can change the world."

Avoid indecision about your vision.

Aspire for precision in your vision.

Accept God's provision for your vision.

At the Ministers Conference in Branson, Missouri, in 2010, Rev. Ryan Ralston said, "God's will is God's bill."

You were called to do the work. The gates of hell shall not prevail. Be a visionary!

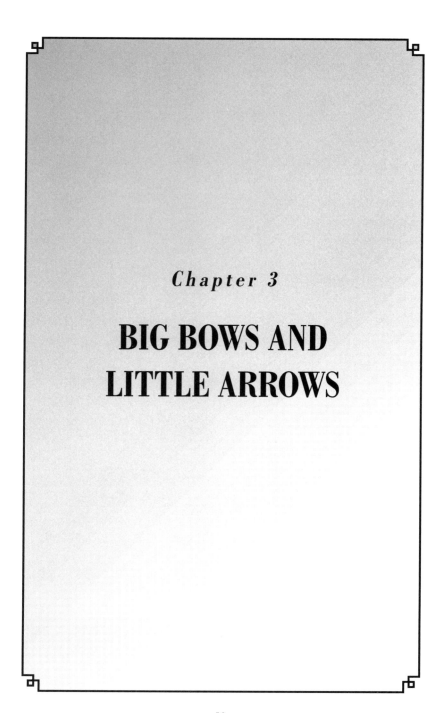

Chapter 3

BIG BOWS AND
LITTLE ARROWS

As arrows are in the hand of a mighty man; so are children of the youth.

—Psalm 127:4 (KJV)

As one looks at this text, it is easy to understand that the children are the "little arrows." Parents must come to grips with the solemn reality that they are the "big bows." Consider the arrow. Within itself, it has no way to find the target; it must be propelled and aimed by the bow! What a great responsibility belongs to parents to aim them in the right direction.

The home is the number-one influence in the life of a child. The average church has a child 1 percent of his time; the home has him 83 percent of his time, and the school for the remaining 16 percent. This does not minimize the need for churches and schools, but it establishes the fact the home is 83 percent of a child's world and parents have only one time around to make it of maximum benefit.

Regarding common trends in today's culture, the attitude of many parents today is as such: *I'm going to let them make their own choice because I have enough of my own problems than to worry about their personal choices. It's their life and their choice! Let them decide*

- *whether they attend church or not;*
- *the kind of music they listen to;*
- *the things they wear;*
- *whether they want unlimited internet in their room or not;*
- *whether they want to post their profiles on a social media site for some pedophile to view; or*
- *whether they want to talk on their cell phone all hours of the night!*

A good father does not give everything a child asks for. A Danish proverb notes, "Give in to a pig when it grunts and a child when he cries, and you will have a fine pig and a bad child." The Lord wants His people to raise children who are godly and productive, not worldly and entitled.

Parenting without setting forth guidelines is dangerous! Inconsistencies will kill children! Proverbs 29:15 says, "The rod and reproof give wisdom: but a child left to himself bringeth his mother to shame" (KJV).

This could be illustrated by the following examples:

- A rattlesnake is in a child's bedroom. One may say, "It's your decision if you want to sleep there or not."
- A child rides a bike in the middle of a four-lane highway. One may say, "Do whatever you think is best."
- Children are playing on the edge of the Grand Canyon, and one responds by saying, "We don't want to brainwash you to believe there is danger in this decision to play near the four thousand foot drop-off. You need to learn for yourself."

Some parents are more worried about preserving the temporal body of their child more than their eternal soul! In which direction are the "little arrows" aimed? Do they hear one thing yet are being aimed in another direction?

A pastor and his wife decided to have the church deacons and their wives over for dinner. It was quite an undertaking, but the pastor and his wife wanted to be "salt and light" for the leaders of their church. When it came time for dinner, everyone was seated, and the pastor's wife asked her four-year-old daughter if she would say grace. The girl said, "I don't know what to say." Her mom told her, "Just say what I say, honey." Everyone bowed their heads, and the little girl said, "Oh dear Lord, why am I having all these people over for dinner? Amen!"

The arrow itself does not have the ability to change directions. Arrows fly in a straight line toward the target. Could the life lived before them be giving them reason to doubt the instruction? Dear parent, actions speak much louder than words.

Are they hearing it is

- wrong to steal, yet we rob God of our tithes?
- wrong to kill while character assassination (gossip) ruins influences in their lives?
- wrong to commit adultery, and all the while indulging in soap operas and romance novels?
- wrong to worship idols as the heathen, yet we are more dedicated to our jobs than to Jesus Christ and His kingdom?
- wrong to fornicate outside marriage but allow them watch movies that promote and glorify this type of lifestyle?
- wrong to use profanity, but when we get hot under the collar, a few choice words slip by?

One cannot point their little arrows toward

- secular music, and expect to raise a spiritual man or woman;
- idolatry, and expect them to be an outstanding saint; or
- Hollywood, and expect them to live holy lives.

Children do not have the ability to support such vices. It is the parent who provides the means to allow them exposure to worldliness.

No godly parent wants to raise children to be sports stars, couch potatoes, or entertainers. A godly parent wants to raise children who are filled with the power of God, great laypersons in the local church, and outstanding citizens in their respective communities. This will not happen by accident. As parents, one must have an intentional goal to see their children walk in truth and love the Lord with all their hearts!

It is imperative to ask every day, "Which way am I pointing my little arrows?"

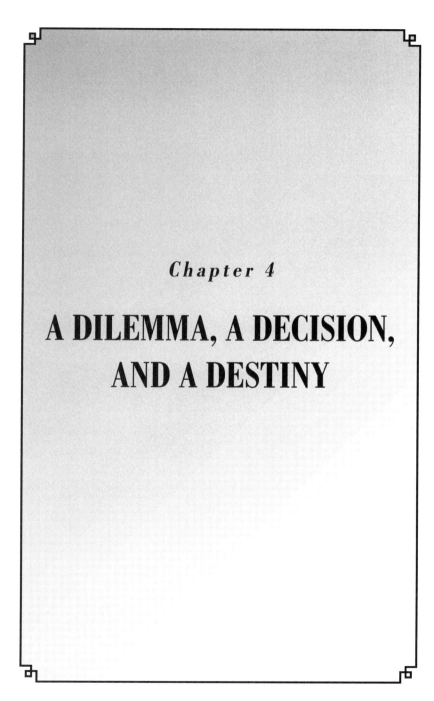

Chapter 4

A DILEMMA, A DECISION, AND A DESTINY

Two hunters came across a bear so big that they dropped their rifles and ran for cover. One man climbed a tree while the other hid in a nearby cave. The bear was in no hurry to eat, so he sat down between the tree and the cave to reflect upon his good fortune. Suddenly, and for no apparent reason, the hunter in the cave came rushing out, almost ran into the waiting bear, hesitated, and then dashed back in again. The same thing happened a second time. When he emerged for the third time, his companion in the tree frantically called out, "Woody, are you crazy? Stay in the cave until he leaves!" "Can't," Woody cried. "There's another bear in there."

Let us examine the story of 1 Kings 17:8–16 in our text.

1. Her Dilemma

In this text we can see this woman has a dilemma, for she said, "As the Lord thy God liveth, I have not a cake, but a handful of meal in a barrel, and a little oil in a cruse: and, behold, I am gathering two sticks, that I may go in and dress it for me and my son, that we may eat it, and die" (KJV).

Many can identify with this woman. In their trouble they

- Do not know how to solve it;
- Do not know how to get over it;
- Do not know how to get beyond it.

They have a dilemma.

Their spiritual eyes have been *blinded* by *bitterness;* spiritual ears have been *deafened* with *discouragement;* and spiritual strength has been *strained* because of the *stress.*

They have a dilemma. Should they lie down, die, and give up because the *valley* has taken their *victory;* the *storm* has *diminished* their *desire;* and the *battle* has *bumped* them off *balance.*

Wait. Before you give in to the *dilemma, remember:* you have a *decision!*

2. Her Decision

In verse 13, the Bible reads, "Elijah said unto her, Fear not; go and do as thou hast said: but make me thereof a little cake first, and bring it unto me, and after make for thee and for thy son." Was the prophet saying to her to put God first even when she thought they were going to die? She had a decision to make: obey God, or feed the flesh.

When we have a *dilemma* it is hard to *deny* the flesh. When we are in the fight, we have a choice to *fall to the flesh or let faith flourish.* We have to be careful not to make a bad decision at a bad time.

How many people make regretful decisions during a low time? A pastor may resign his church. A husband may leave his wife. A family may leave their home church. The bad decision has harmful consequences because the choice was made when he or she was in a wrong frame of mind.

It may be true that there are two sides to every question, but it is also true that there are two sides to a sheet of flypaper. It makes a big difference to the fly which side he chooses.

Pastor James Suits said, "Never make a decision at a low time or you will probably live to regret it."

David Russell said, "The hardest thing to learn in life is which bridge to cross and which to burn."

Robert H. Schuler tells the story that one winter his dad needed firewood. He found a dead tree and sawed it down. In the spring, to his dismay, new shoots sprouted around the trunk. He said, "I thought for sure it was dead. The leaves had all dropped in the wintertime. It was so cold that twigs snapped as if there were no life left in the old tree. But now I see that there was still life at the taproot." He looked at his son and said, "Bob, don't forget this important lesson. Never cut a tree down in the winter."

It is hard to make a good decision when you are scraping the bottom of the barrel. It is hard to do what is right when you are starving and struggling on the inside. It is hard to take a leap of faith when you are lying facedown! Do not quit when you are down. Do not give in when you are out. Do not throw in the towel and give up; hold on for the miracle!

3.   Her Decision Determined Her Destiny

Her decision was that she obeyed God. The Bible says in verses 15 and 16, "And she went and did according to the saying of Elijah: and she, and he, and her house, did eat many days. And the barrel of meal wasted not, neither did the cruse of oil fail, according to the word of the Lord, which he spake by Elijah" (KJV).

Your decision will determine whether your destiny is

- life or death
- victory or failure
- heaven or hell
- saved or lost
- bondage or freedom
- happiness or horror
- peace or misery
- grace or judgment
- beauty or bitterness
- salvation or sin

In your dilemma, you must make a decision that will determine your destiny.

Harry S. Truman said, "Men who live in the past remind me of a toy you have seen. The toy is a small wooden bird called the 'Floogie Bird.' Around the Floogie Bird's neck is a label reading, 'I fly backwards, I don't care where I'm going. I just want to see where I've been.'"

You cannot dwell on past problem; we must focus on faith for the future. Just like the man we find in Mark 2:3, who was sick of the palsy his dilemma was sickness, his decision was to go to Jesus, his destiny was to be made whole by the power of God. Sin says, "You make your bed, now lie in it," but Jesus says, "Take up thy bed and walk."

My dear friend, let us remember: destiny is not a matter of chance. It is a matter of choice!

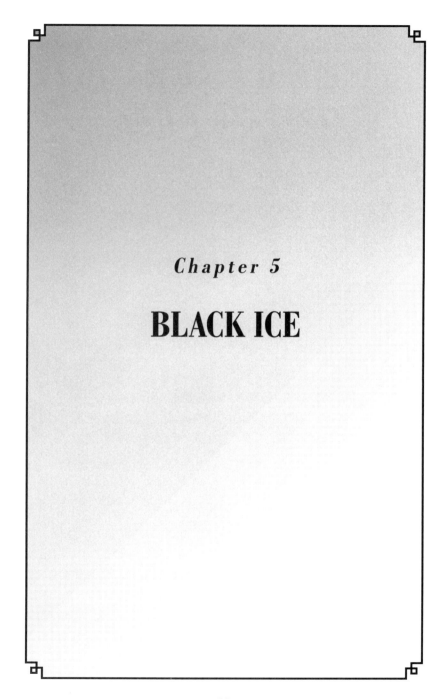

Chapter 5

BLACK ICE

Which are blackish by reason of the ice, and wherein the snow is hid.

—Job 6:16 (KJV)

Webster Dictionary says black ice is a thin, nearly invisible layer of ice on a paved road. Old timers identified danger spots where the ice would be thin and unable to hold weight as they crossed a river or lake, and they called it *black ice*.

Although we know in Job's time blacktop did not exist, yet the concept of black ice was found in the life of this great man.

In one day, Job lost

- seven thousand sheep
- three thousand camels
- five hundred yoke of oxen
- five hundred asses
- four children

He experienced an unexpected upheaval. Job knew about the *black ice* of life!

In the 1990s my wife and I were traveling from Richmond, Indiana, to Bro. James Parrot's church for a fellowship meeting in Connersville, Indiana. The route we traveled was Indiana State Rd. 1. Just as we were coming into town, the car in front of us began to swerve out of control. The roads had been clear the entire trip, so I thought it was a teenager playing around. I began to laugh and brag about my driving skills to my wife. All at once, with no warning at all, we began to spin out of control. A fire hydrant next to the road had been leaking, and with the temperature being subzero, there was black ice all over that particular stretch of road. It hit fast and furious!

It is our nature to sit back and observe someone else who is slipping on the black ice of life and be unconcerned or vocalize what we would do and how we would handle the situation. We must be careful. It is different when it is you. Remember the proverb that says, "Never criticize someone until you've walked a mile in his or her shoes."

Every one of us must travel the road of life, and we do not know when or where, but sooner or later we will come across the black ice of life. You are going along minding your own business and then *wham!*

Everything seems

- to spin out of control—slipping out of control;
- blindsided by calamity—never saw it coming!

If you had known it was coming, you could have

- handled it;
- braced yourself;
- been ready;
- prepared for it.

But that is not how black ice works! It's unexpected.

I know what black ice is.

- I've heard the words out of the doctor's mouth, "We think your wife has cancer." She was in her twenties, and we hit black ice.

- I've heard the doctor say, "We don't think your ten-day-old baby will make it. He has RSV." (RSV is respiratory syncytial virus, a serious infection.) We hit black ice.
- I've heard the doctor say to me, "You have either MS or you've had a stroke." I was in my twenties. I hit black ice.

One morning I received a phone call from my dad, Rev. Doug Webb. I could tell by his vocal tones he was upset. He told me that my aunt Sheeree had passed away in the night. How could this be? My aunt and I were three years apart in age and close friends. We did everything together. She always bought me a special birthday gift. She was only thirty. Friend, I have experienced "black ice" of life.

When you get to those times, you need God to take control of your life. There was a pastor named Steve who was traveling around Christmastime … I'll let him tell it to you in his own words.

> Steve clutched the side of his seat, eyes wide in disbelief. There was no way they could make an emergency landing when visibility between the plane and the control tower was completely cut off by the fog.
>
> He opened the maps, and Joe estimated their location. According to the map, they should be directly above the airport. Gradually, Joe began to descend through the fog toward the ground. As he did, the voice of the controller entered the cockpit. "Pull it up! Pull it up!" They were not over the airport as they had thought. Instead,

they were over a busy interstate highway and had missed an overpass by no more than five feet.

At that instant, the controller's voice broke the silence again. "If you will listen to me, I'll help you get down," he said. "Go ahead. I'm listening." Steve closed his eyes momentarily and prayed, begging God to guide them safely through the fog onto the ground. Meanwhile, the controller began guiding Joe toward a landing. "Come down a little. Okay, a little more. Not that much. All right, now over to the right. Straighten it out and come down a little more."

The calm, reassuring voice of the controller continued its steady stream of directions, and Joe, intent on the voice, did as he was instructed. The trip seemed to take an eternity, and he wondered whether he would see his wife again.

The controller continued. "Raise it a little more. Okay, you're too far to the left. That's right. Now lower it a little more. All right, you're right over the end of the runway. Set it down. Now!"

Carefully responding just as he was told, Joe lowered the plane, and when he was a few feet from the ground, the runway came into sight. As the plane touched down, Steve saw Katy standing nearby waiting for him, and his eyes filled with tears of relief and gratitude. The two men in the cockpit looked at each other. Without saying a word, they bowed their heads and closed their eyes. "Thank you, God," Steve said, his voice choked with emotion.

Joe picked up the plane's radio and contacted the control tower. "Hey, I just want to thank you for what you did. We couldn't have made it without those directions."

There was a brief pause. "What are you talking about?" the controller asked. He had a different voice this time, and he was clearly confused. "We lost all radio contact with you when we told you to return to Pierre."

Goose bumps rose up on Steve's arms, and he watched as Joe's face went blank in disbelief. "You what?" he asked.

"We never heard from you again, and we never heard you talking to us or to anyone else," the controller said.

"We were stunned when we saw you break through the clouds right over the runway. It was a perfect landing."—K. Kingsbury, *A Treasure of Christmas Miracles*

My friend, when you do not know what to do and you hit the black ice of life, let the voice of the Father lead you to safety.

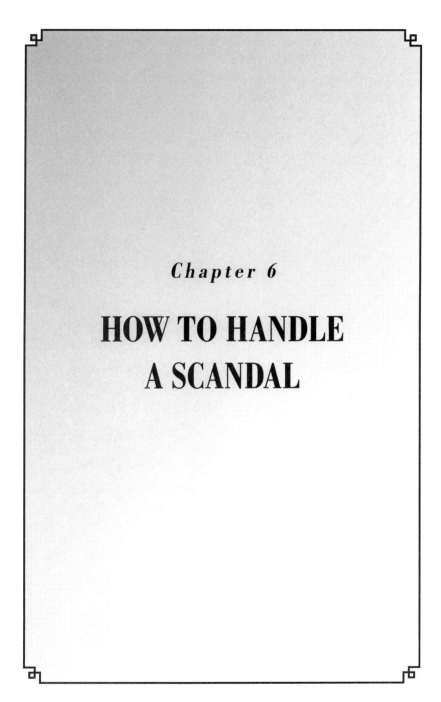

Chapter 6

HOW TO HANDLE
A SCANDAL

1 Chronicles 10: 7–13 (KJV)

This is a sad, sad story about a fallen man. Saul was raised up by Almighty God. He was revered and honored among his brethren. The hand of God rested upon him as he led the Israelites. This king was head and shoulders above all of Israel; therefore, they all looked up to him. But there was a day when he did his own thing; it ended in catastrophe. A dark cloud of disobedience settled on Saul's soul, and the lights went out. The man of God had given him specific instructions to totally destroy the Amalekites. When the prophet Samuel came into camp after the battle was seemingly won, he heard the sound of the spoil. The old prophet said, "What meaneth the bleating of the sheep in my ears."

Have you ever heard something and your heart falls; a sick feeling overtakes you as you grieve that someone has been disobedient to God? The Bible said in 1 Samuel 15:26, "And Samuel said unto Saul, I will not return with thee: for thou hast rejected the word of the Lord, and the Lord hath rejected thee from being king over Israel." It is amazing that even though Saul and Samuel were close, the man of God did not pull any punches or play politics. He could not be bought. He was God's man!

Now most Bible scholars say that Saul reigned for forty-two years. They say this failure was early on; however, God did not remove him for forty years. When a skeleton comes out of the closet that has been unknown for years, questions arise, like,

"How in the world could they be living like that, us not know it, and they retain their position for that long?" We feel violated and taken.

However, there came a day of judgment, a reckoning day of sorts, as 1 Samuel 31:9 said of Saul, "And they cut off his head, and stripped off his armor, and sent into the land of the Philistines round about, to publish it in the house of their idols, and among the people" (KJV).

There will be a day of judgment, but we must let God bring it about. There are two ways to handle scandal as shown in our text. There is the way of the heathen. They took his head and his armor and sent into the land of the Philistines roundabout to publish it in the house of their idols and among the people. They wanted everybody to know the mighty had fallen. It gave the enemies of God opportunity to blaspheme. It gave all the skeptics around town opportunity to say, "We knew those people of God were odd, now look at their shame!"

Consider this: take 2 Samuel 1:25 literally as it is written in its context, "How are the mighty fallen." This statement is finished with an exclamation mark as expressing grief, pain, sorrow, and regret by making a statement. Why do so many tend to put a question mark there? "How are the mighty fallen?" What are the dirty details? Who can I call who has not heard? What do I need to know about this situation? Please excuse me if I'm too blunt, but there are some things we don't need to know. If it is not our business, do not make it our business.

A minister in Arkansas shared a story with me about how his pastor handled a scandal. Years ago there had been a some talk concerning a situation in the church. The pastor stood up in service and said, "I know some of you have been talking. Shut up! You think you know, but you do not!" That was the end of it. *That is how to handle a scandal!*

Fellow Christians, we should not have a hotline to share all the juicy gossip. You will ruin yourself if you partake in such nonsense. Some folks regularly have a social media revelation. They get their info from "tell-all Twitter"—and then we have the FBI: Facebook Investigators—meandering through fields of followers and friends just so they know what everybody has done.

We are following Jesus, who has never failed. We should be committed to sharing His good news. We do not feed our souls on a bitter backslider's post that is publishing his sins for the whole world to see. What spiritual uplift is that? It is the way of the heathen. We are not bottom feeders! We do not ingest the junk of this world. We are the children of the King! We feed on the daily bread of God's Word.

God's people handle the scandal differently than the heathen. Let us look at these men of Jabesh Giliad. "And when all Jabesh Gilead heard all that the Philistines had done to Saul, They arose, all the valiant men, and took away the body of Saul, and the bodies of his sons, and brought them to Jabesh, and buried their bones under the oak in Jabesh, and fasted seven days" (KJV).

They handled it properly.

One of the things that sets one apart as a man or woman of God is how one handles scandal. God's people do not sweep sin under the rug. Nor do they air out everybody's dirty laundry.

They do not ignore or explore sin. Christians do not pet sin, nor do we publicize it. We do not brush off failure, but we do not broadcast it to the world. There is something horribly wrong with people who gloat in and broadcast others' failures. When I was a child I overheard a minister, concerning a fallen fellow camp meeting minister, say, "Well, I guess we will all have a chance to preach some big meetings now." What a selfish attitude. He should have been weeping over the loss of a brother and the loss of confidence of the people. Proverbs 11:13 says, "A talebearer revealeth secrets: but he that is of a faithful spirit concealeth the matter" (KJV).

Brethren, there is right way and a wrong way to handle a scandal.

Publicize or privatize.

We can stir the pot under the cover of prayer request. Remember, when you stir up something dead, it stinks! We can throw gasoline on the fire or be a fire extinguisher. Deal with it, and then let it be buried underneath the precious blood of Jesus.

> There is a right way to handle a scandal.
> What a Friend we have in Jesus,
> All our sins and griefs to bear!
> What a privilege to carry
> Everything to God in prayer!
> O what peace we often forfeit,
> O what needless pain we bear,
> All because we do not carry
> Everything to God in prayer!
> —Joseph M. Scriven

Chapter 7

OUR CHILDREN'S BEHAVIOR

2 Samuel 12:14

A group of expectant fathers were in a waiting room while their wives were in the process of delivering babies. A nurse came in and announced to one man that his wife had just given birth to twins. "That's quite a coincidence," he responded. "I play for the Minnesota Twins!" A few minutes later, another nurse came in and announced to another man that he was the father of triplets. "That's amazing," he exclaimed. "I work for the 3M Company." At that point, a third man slipped off his chair and lay on the floor. Somebody asked him if he was feeling ill. "I'm starting to," he responded. "I happen to work for the 7-Up Company."

2 Samuel 12:14 tells us, "Howbeit, because by this deed thou hast given great occasion to the enemies of the LORD to blaspheme" (KJV).

I must admit, although I have four wonderful children who are all saved and baptized in the Holy Ghost, I do not have it all figured out, and they are not perfect. As John Wilmot, Earl of Rochester, said, "Before I got married I had six theories about bringing up children; now I have six children and no theories."

Author Owen Wister, an old college friend of Theodore Roosevelt, was visiting the president at the White House. Roosevelt's daughter Alice kept running in and out of the room until Wister finally asked if there was something Roosevelt could do to control her. "Well," said the president, "I can do one of two things. I can be president of the United States, or I can control Alice. I cannot possibly do both." It would be easy to pawn our responsibilities on to someone else. I fear many of our young parents make an excuse that we cannot control our children's actions because we have *much greater responsibilities.*

Dear mom and dad: there is no job that needs to be completed, no music that needs to be played, no song that needs to be sung, no message that needs to be delivered above the God-called duty to teach our own children. As the word teaches us, what would it profit a man if he gained the whole world and lose his own soul? Children are naturally restless, wigglers, unruly, independent, and selfish. We must remember they are ours and our responsibility.

We must not allow our children to be selfish. The first thing they learn to say is "mine." May I offer the "property laws of a toddler"? Some might say that this is evidences of original sin.

1. If I like it, it is mine.
2. If it is in my hand, it is mine.
3. If I can take it from you, it is mine.
4. If I had it a little while ago, it is mine.
5. If it is mine, it must never appear to be yours in any way.
6. If I am doing or building something, all the pieces are mine.
7. If it looks just like mine, it is mine.
8. If I saw it first, it is mine.
9. If you are playing with something and you put it down, it automatically becomes mine.
10. If it is broken, it is yours.

Here are three important points for parents.

1. Be Aware

A young mother, paying a visit to the home of friends who were both scientists, made no attempt to restrain her five-year-old son, who was ransacking an adjoining room. Finally, an extra-loud clatter of bottles did prompt her to say, "I hope you don't mind Johnny being in there."

"No," the chemist calmly said, "he'll be quiet when he gets to the poisons."

Sometimes our children surprise us and catch us off guard by acting up at an inopportune time. We must depend on the Lord to give us patience and wisdom in those moments.

It is commonly spoken among restaurant staff that church people offer the most complaints, make the most demands, and leave the smallest tips. The other thing is that the unruly children of so-called church parents climb over booths, spill drinks, throw food on the floor, and talk or scream at rude levels while mom and dad act *oblivious*. After leaving a two dollar tip (10 percent of the bill), the remnants of little "Hurricane Katrina" are strewn all over the floor, and the server is dead on her feet, they have the audacity to invite people to church. *If this was the only example of Christ that a person would ever see, what would he or she think of Him?*

2. The Responsibility

A pastor once had an evangelist and his family over to his house for a time of fellowship. He had just had the house painted for his wife. One of the evangelist's children decided the wall needed a hole in it, so he took a baseball bat and dented in the walls. The evangelist looked at the pastor and said, "Whatever he tears up I'll pay to have repaired."

Ladies and gentlemen, may I submit to you that there was something else that needed to be torn up. Dad needed to point the child's feet toward the north pole, his head toward the south pole, and warm up the equator. Christian parent, whatever your kids tear up, mess up, break, or borrow, make sure it is taken care of.

We must make sure in our discipline that as parents, we never let the child play on our sympathy. If they get in trouble with mom, they should also be in trouble with dad and vice versa. We should never let a child undermine the authority of the parent who is disciplining at the moment.

The story is told of a little boy sitting on his front steps with his face cradled in his hands, looking so forlorn. His dad came home and asked him what was wrong. The little boy looked up and said, "Well, just between us, Dad, I'm having trouble getting along with your wife too!"

According to psychologist William Damon, respect for the parent who exercises proper authority leads to respect for legitimate social institutions and respect for law. In his book *The Moral Child*, Damon writes, "The child's respect for parental authority sets the direction for civilized participation in the social order when the child later begins assuming the rights and responsibilities of full citizenship." Damon calls this respect "the single most important legacy that could be left to them."

We should teach our children to treat their siblings right. A Sunday school teacher was discussing the Ten Commandments with her five- and six-year-olds. After explaining the commandment to honor thy father and thy mother, she asked, "Is there a commandment that teaches us how to treat our brothers and sisters?" Without missing a beat, one little boy answered, "Thou shall not kill."

3. A Home Should be a Haven from Animosity

> If a child lives with criticism,
> He learns to condemn.
> If a child lives with hostility
> He learns to fight.
> If a child lives with ridicule,
> He learns to be shy.
> If a child lives with shame,
> He learns to feel guilty.
> If a child lives with tolerance,
> He learns to be patient.
> If a child lives with encouragement,
> He learns confidence.
> If a child lives with praise,
> He learns to appreciate.
> If a child lives with fairness,
> He learns justice.
> If a child lives with security,
> He learns to have faith.
> If a child lives with approval,
> He learns to like himself.
> If a child lives with acceptance and friendship,
> He learns to find love in the world.

—Dorothy Law Nolte

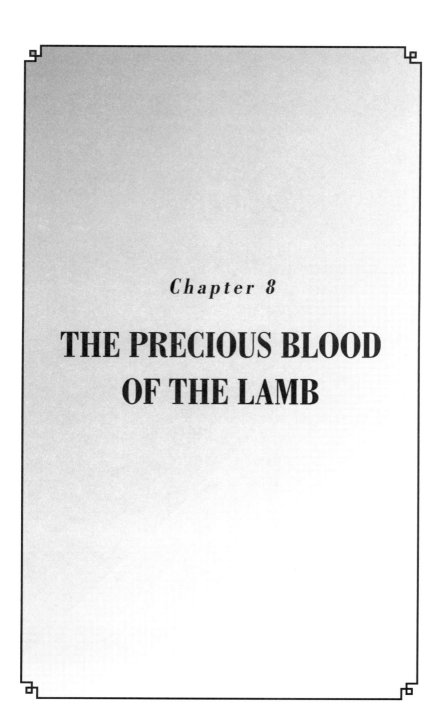

Chapter 8

THE PRECIOUS BLOOD
OF THE LAMB

And they overcame him by the blood of the Lamb.

—Revelation 12:11 (KJV)

W. D. Davies states in his book *Paul and Rabbinic Judaism* that in the temple at Jerusalem every year, there were many sacrifices. There were 1,093 lambs, 113 bulls, 37 rams, and 32 goats. These were the official sacrifices and did not count the private sacrifices of the people! These sacrifices pacified God but did not satisfy Him. However, there was a lamb—a spotless lamb. He was the Lamb of God slain from the foundation of the earth.

One of President Lyndon B. Johnson's daughters was once asked by an inquisitive journalist to describe her relationship with her famous father. Without a moment's hesitation she replied, "Blood."

May I submit to you that when I was a sinner, it was not

- singing that saved me—*it was the blood!*
- my last name that cleansed me—*it was the blood!*
- the Virgin Mary that atoned for my sins—*it was the blood!*
- the water in a creek that washed away my sin—*it was the blood!*
- shaking of the preacher's hand or becoming a member that lifted me from hell's flames—*it was the blood!*

The blood is

- the sin eradicator;
- the soul emancipator;
- the addiction eliminator.

The blood is

- the curse crusher;
- the conscience clearer;
- the carnality cleanser.

The blood is

- Satan's thorn;
- sinners' trust'
- saints' triumph.

The blood is

- Calvary's cleanser;
- Heaven's mender;
- a broken life changer.

About the blood:

- Demons dread the thought of it;
- Hell shakes at the sight of it;
- Redeemed rejoice at the wonder of it.

Are you washed in the blood?

An alcoholic became a believer and was asked how he could possibly believe all the nonsense in the Bible about miracles. "You don't believe Jesus changed the water into wine, do you?" He answered confidently, "I sure do, because in our house Jesus changed the whiskey into furniture."

The devil has lied to millions. He convinces them there is no hope, that they have gone too far and done too much, but there is an answer written in the Word of God that refutes this thinking. It is found in 1 John 1:7: "and the blood of Jesus Christ his son cleanseth us from all sin."

At thirty-two years of age, William Cowper (1731–1800) passed through a great crisis in his life. He tried to end his life by taking laudanum. Then he hired a coach and was driven to the Thames, intending to throw himself into the river; but some power seemed to restrain him. The next morning he fell upon a knife, but the blade broke and his life was saved. He then tried to hang himself and was cut down unconscious but still alive. One morning, in a moment of strange cheerfulness, he took up his Bible and read a verse in the letter to the Romans. He suddenly received strength to believe and rejoiced in the forgiving power of God. Some years later, after he had passed through a rich Christian experience and had written many beautiful hymns, Cowper sat down one day and summed up his faith in God's dealings with him. He then penned these timeless words: "There is a fountain filled with blood drawn from Emmanuel's veins, and sinners plunged beneath the flood lose all their guilty stains!"

As was said by the Reverend Shad McDonald at the 2011 Pentecostal Fire Youth Conference in Louisville, Kentucky: "I believe the blood of the Lamb

- atones and assures
- bought and blesses
- cleanses and consecrates
- delivers and delights
- emancipates and eradicates
- frees and furnishes
- glorious and great

- healing and holy
- immaculate and infinite
- just and justified
- kingly and keeping
- lovely and loosing
- marvelous and mysterious
- necessary and noble
- obliterates and overcomes
- pardons and purifies
- quickens and qualifies
- redeems and revives
- saves and sanctifies
- trustworthy and triumphant
- unadulterated and unequal
- valuable and vital
- worthy and wonderful

Because of the blood I am an ex-sinner because He was yielded up a perfect sacrifice who took away my sins, which were zillions!"

The condition of your soul may be weighing heavy. The rest you seek escapes you, but listen my friend … call on Jesus, repent of your sins, and find forgiveness and peace in Jesus.

A preacher once said, "God can save anybody, anywhere, anytime!"

In Matthew 19:25 the disciples asked, "Who then can be saved?" Thank God anyone can be saved.

Anybody.

- He saved a harlot named Rahab.
- He saved a demon-possessed woman like Mary Magdalene.
- He saved a religious man like Nicodemus.
- He saved a rich man like Zacchaeus.
- He saved a poor man like Lazarus.
- He saved a fisherman like Peter.
- He saved a doctor like Luke.
- He saved a government official like the Ethiopian.
- He saved a lawyer like Zenas.
- He saved a jailer like the Philippian.
- He saved the thief who was hanging on a cross.
- He saved a tax collector like Matthew

In the Bible there is no white church, black church, red church, yellow church, or brown church. There is only the blood-bought church of Jesus Christ. Jesus did not come to save skins but souls!

- He saved Levi in a tax office (Mark 2:14).
- He saved Peter and Andrew at work.
- He saved the paralytic man in a house.
- He saved Zacchaeus at the foot of a tree (Luke 19:4).
- He saved Paul in the middle of the road (Acts 9:3).
- He saved the Samaritan woman at a well (John 4:11).
- He saved the Ethiopian in the desert (Acts 8:26).
- He saved the Philippian jailer in a prison (Acts 16:26).
- He saved the thief on a cross (Matthew 27:38).
- He saved Legion in a graveyard.

Whether you are on the job, at home, up a tree, in the middle of the road, at a well, in a desert, in prison, or on a cross, Jesus has the ability to save anyone, anywhere.

Anytime.

- The apostle Paul testified that he was saved at "midday."
- The thief on the cross was saved between the sixth and ninth hour.
- Nicodemus was saved at "night" (John 3:2).
- The Philippian jailer was saved at "midnight" (Acts 16:25).

Because of the blood, He can save anybody, anywhere, anytime.

"But what saith it? The word is nigh thee, even in thy mouth, and in thy heart: that is, the word of faith, which we preach; That if thou shalt confess with thy mouth the Lord Jesus, and shalt believe in thine heart that God hath raised him from the dead, thou shalt be saved" (Romans 10:8–9 KJV).

Chapter 9

THE IMPORTANCE OF MUSIC IN THE CHURCH

Praise him with the sound of the trumpet: praise him with the psaltery and harp. Praise him with the timbrel and dance: praise him with stringed instruments and organs. Praise him upon the loud cymbals: praise him upon the high sounding cymbals.

—Psalm 150:3–5 (KJV)

Martin Luther said, "The devil takes flight at the sound of music, just as he does at the words of theology, and for this reason the prophets always combined theology and music, the teaching of truth and the chanting of Psalms and hymns." He also said, "After theology, I give the highest place and greatest honor to music."

I love preaching. I also love singing and music. When we peer into the future of eternity, we see no biblical foretelling that there will be preaching in heaven. As a matter of fact, singing and playing music is some of the only things that we do here on this earth that we will also do in heaven.

Some believe music is not a ministry; it is strictly entertainment. Music can be entertainment when the focus is on people. But music can also be ministry. My mind goes back to the example in the Bible when David played cunningly on his harp and drove the evil spirits away from King Saul. I have seen many hardened sinners, who would not break after hearing a sermon, come weeping down the aisle when hearing a good old gospel song.

Our singing must lift up Christ. Bro. Gary Hampton said, "If music appeals to your flesh rather than your spirit, it cannot be godly."

The great composer Bach said, "All music should have no other end aim than the glory of God and the soul's refreshment; where this is not remembered there is no real music but only a devilish hubbub." He headed his compositions: "JJ"—"Jesus

Juva," which means "Jesus help me." He ended them "SDG"—
"Soli Dei gratia," which means "To God alone the praise."

The Gold City Quartet released "Somebody Sing Me a Gospel
Song" in 2012, and the lyric stated this:

> Somebody sing me a gospel song.
> Tell me again that God's love is strong,
> And I'm forgiven for what I've done wrong.
> Somebody sing me a gospel song.

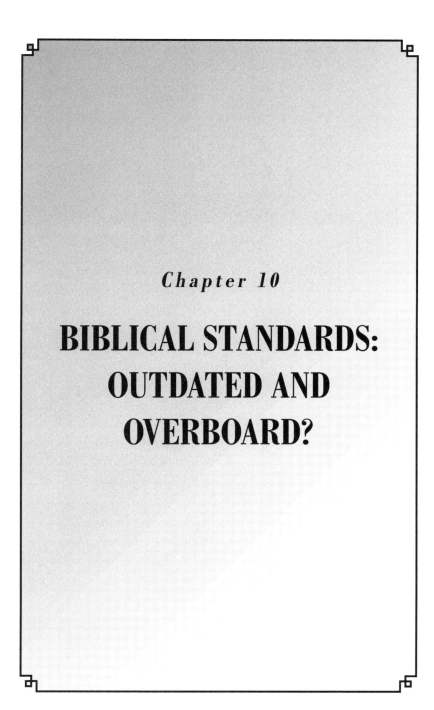

Chapter 10

BIBLICAL STANDARDS: OUTDATED AND OVERBOARD?

But as he which hath called you is holy, so be ye holy in all manner of conversation; Because it is written, Be ye holy; for I am holy.

—1 Peter 1:15–16 (KJV)

This chapter references 2 Corinthians 7:1; 2 Corinthians 6:17; and Hebrews 12:14

There is a growing movement that feels biblical holiness standards are out of style, outdated, and irrelevant. This sermon is not crafted to list standards, for they are listed in the Bible. The intent is to help us understand the importance of having standards.

Why do we need standards? Are we not in the dispensation of grace? Surely the days of legalism are over, but wait! Should we not read the words of Jesus Christ Himself? "Think not that I am come to destroy the law, or the prophets: I am not come to destroy, but to fulfil" (Matthew 5:17).

My dear friend, when asked about divorce and remarriage, Christ said in Matthew 5:27–28, "Ye have heard that it was said by them of old time, Thou shalt not commit adultery: But I say unto you, That whosoever looketh on a woman to lust after her hath committed adultery with her already in his heart."

Christ did not loosen the level of requirement under grace, he tightened it down. *It's like this. The only people who are mad about the truth are those living a lie!*

If standards are not important … go to the gas station for a fill-up. You will find a sticker on the pump that reads "This pump has been examined and approved by the Dept. of Agriculture and meets the standards of weights and measures." If the pump read that it gave you one gallon of fuel but had really only pumped half a gallon into your tank, *would standards be important?*

Need a shirt? Go to Dillard's and ask the attendant for your size. Suppose they didn't use standard measurement. Take the clothing item home and remove the packaging. Try it on. Hmmm. Could it be that you're busting the buttons? Or on the contrary, it may hang like a tent. *Standards anyone?*

Take a trip to McDonalds and order a super-sized soda. Pay the attendant at the window for the drink and in return they hand you an eight-ounce drink. *Now tell me standards don't matter.*

Let a person who has killed someone be sentenced to thirty years in prison, but the jailer decides it does not matter what the judge says and lets him out in a week. Perhaps the killer moves on next to you. *Are we getting the picture yet?*

Make an apple pie. The recipe says to add a pinch of salt, but instead you are opposed to someone telling you how much salt to use. Who needs standards anyway? So the Morton's box is turned over and poured out *to your liking*. I can guarantee one thing. If you do not adhere to the standard, *the pie will not be to your liking!*

Standards are everywhere. Without standards, our society would not function. A standard is a document established that provides rules, guidelines, or characteristics for products, services, or systems. Simple things we take for granted, from traffic signals to units of measurement, are the same from one place to another thanks to standards.

One of the most misrepresented scriptures in the Bible is 1 Samuel 16:7: "for the Lord seeth not as man seeth; for man looketh on the outward appearance, but the Lord looketh on the heart."

Listen, it is wonderful that your heart is clean, but people cannot see your heart! How are we to be a witness to the world if we look like the world? If our lives do not change after we get saved, what was the reason Christ died? The reason we are called *Christians* is because we are *Christlike*! If we are to be Christlike, we must live up to the standards of biblical holiness.

If 99 percent was good enough, we would get the following:

- No phone service for fifteen minutes each day;
- 1.7 million pieces of first class mail lost each day;
- Thirty-five thousand newborn babies dropped by doctors or nurses each year;
- Two hundred thousand people getting the wrong drug prescriptions each year;
- Unsafe drinking water three days a year;
- Two million people would die from food poisoning each year.

There is an old song that says, "Lord I'm striving, trying to make a hundred ... 99 ½ won't do."

For us to compare ourselves to others and say "I am more conservative than they are," or "my beliefs are stricter than his"—does that make us holy? Wait, wait, wait! We cannot compare ourselves among ourselves. The Bible says those who do so are not wise. The standard for Christian living is the Word of GOD, not people!

Years ago a man used to walk by a jewelry store, stop, and set his watch by the big clock in the window. One day the jeweler happened to be standing in his doorway. He greeted the man in a friendly way and said, "I see you set your watch by my clock. What kind of work do you do that demands such correct time each day?"

"I'm the watchman at the plant down the street. My job is to blow the five o'clock whistle."

The jeweler was startled. "But you can't do that," he blurted. "I set my clock by your whistle!"

Many churches in today's society do not want to deal with people's pet sins. They are repulsed at the final authority (Bible) being used as the "rulebook" for Christian living. They do not want to hear the truth. They want a sermon on love and to hear they are all going to heaven when they die. Never mind their sin.

J. M. Boice said, "You know what Mason said to Dixon? You've got to draw the line somewhere."

If we do not draw the line somewhere, what will we have in twenty years?

- How much worldliness will be in our churches?
- What will our grandchildren believe?
- What percentage of the congregation will have Hollywood elites spewing into their living room?
- Who will preach in our pulpits and sing in our choirs?

- Will we have movie parties for the youth group in the fellowship hall because this new generation has been raised with them undercover in their home right now?
- Will the women let their glory grow, or will it be found on the floor of a beauty salon?
- Will the men look clean-cut?
- Will we have tongue rings, nose rings, eyebrow rings, finger rings?
- Will we have couples living together before marriage?
- Will we be tolerant or possibly embracing of alternate lifestyles?
- Will there be a midweek service?
- Will we still have an altar?
- Will we accept abortion as a choice?
- Will we have contemporary gospel rock worship openly in this sanctuary that all started on our youth groups' iPods?
- Will we be able to have revivals that last longer than a weekend?
- Will we have Super Bowl parties in place of Sunday evening service?
- Will we wear our shorts to church outings?
- Will we permit tattoos and paint ourselves like Jezebel?
- Will our children even know a real move of the Holy Ghost?
- Will we have a form of godliness but deny the power and have "Ichabod" over the church door?

God Forbid!

"Remove not the ancient landmark, which thy fathers have set" (Proverbs 22:28).

Where do we draw the line? Where the Bible draws it!

Who set the standards? God has set them in His Word!

Who is right and who is wrong?

"yea, let God be true, but every man a liar" (Romans 3:4).

Outdated and overboard? Never!

Chapter 11

USE BUT NOT ABUSE

And they that use this world, as not abusing it: for the fashion of this world passeth away.

—1 Corinthians 7:31

It is hard to imagine life without smartphones. For many Americans, it is the first thing they see when waking and the last thing they check before falling asleep. *Fortune* magazine reports that 71 percent of adult Americans sleep with their cell phones next to their beds. A majority text or talk while driving. Twenty percent use their phone during church services. Some take selfies with the dearly departed at funerals. So is there such a thing as cell phone addiction? Yes, there is.

Cell phone addiction is in the same family as other technology addictions, such as computers and gaming. They are all part of a larger family of behavioral addictions (e.g., gambling, exercise, etc.) Anything that can produce pleasure in the serotonin level in your brain has the potential to become addictive. Loss of control is the essential element of any addiction.

Research has identified the six signs of any type of substance or behavioral addiction. Those six signs—salience, mood modification, tolerance, withdrawal, conflict, and relapse—apply to cell phone addiction as well.

Are you addicted?

Read the definitions of each of the six signs below and then agree or disagree with the following statements. By the time you have completed this task, you will have a better idea of whether you have reached your tipping point when it comes to your cell phone use.

Salience

A behavior becomes salient when it is deeply integrated into your daily routine.

- The first thing I reach for after waking in the morning is my cell phone.
- I would turn around and go back home on the way to work if I had left my cell phone at home.

Euphoria

Who knows what the beep, buzz, whistle, or stylized ringtone might have in store for you? The feeling of anticipation or excitement that precedes and/or follows the use of your cell phone is a mood modification that can result in euphoria.

- I often use my cell phone when I am bored.
- I have pretended to take calls to avoid awkward social situations.

Tolerance

As in the case of drug and alcohol abuse, tolerance addresses the need for an ever-increasing "dose" of the behavior to achieve the desired "high."

- I find myself spending more and more time on my cell phone.
- I spend more time than I should on my cell phone and feel guilty for using it so much.

Withdrawal symptoms

The feelings of irritability, stress, anxiousness, desperation, and even panic that often occur when you are separated from your cell phone are good examples of withdrawal symptoms.

- I become agitated or irritable when my cell phone is out of sight.
- I have gone into a panic when I thought I had lost my cell phone.

Conflict

A common outcome of cell phone addiction is conflict. Does your spouse or children complain that you are always on your phone? Do you allow texts, calls, and emails to spoil your vacations and personal time? Are your work activities interrupted by playing games, visiting Facebook, and countless other forms of entertainment offered on your cell phone?

- I have argued with my spouse, friends, or family about my cell phone use.
- I use my cell phone while driving my car.

Relapse

When we acknowledge that our cell phone use may be undermining our well-being, we attempt to stop, but then we slip back. We relapse.

- I have tried to curb my cell phone use, but the effort did not last very long.
- I need to reduce my cell phone use, but am afraid I cannot do it.

Are you addicted? It is time to see if you have crossed the tipping point from reasonable cell phone use to a potentially addictive habit. To calculate your score, simply add up the number of "agree" responses to each of the twelve statements and check the results.

8+ "Agrees": You are addicted.

5–7 "Agrees": You have crossed the tipping point and are moving quickly to full-blown cell phone addiction.

3–4 "Agrees": You have not yet reached your tipping point, but need to carefully assess how your cell phone is influencing your life.

0–2 "Agrees": You are living a disciplined life.

I know we need to use, but let's not abuse!

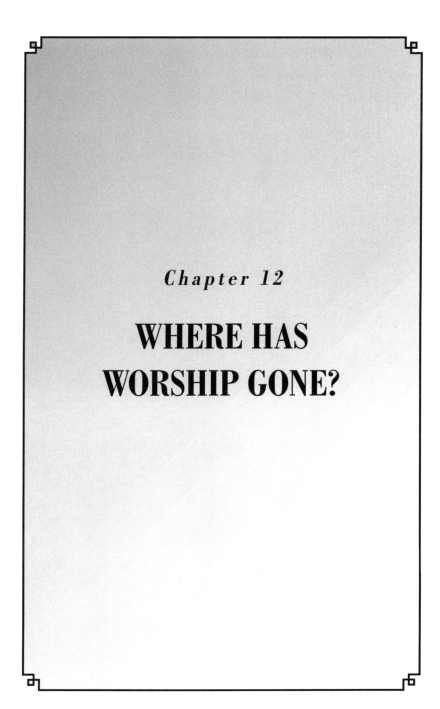

Chapter 12

WHERE HAS
WORSHIP GONE?

But the hour cometh, and now is, when the true worshippers shall worship the Father in spirit and in truth: for the Father seeketh such to worship him.

—John 4:23 (KJV)

Where has worship gone? As a child, I remember countless times waking up from a catnap under the church pew, heels clomping and bobby pins skidding across the hardwood floor of Calvary Holiness Church in Brooks, Kentucky. It was part of what we did. It was who we were. The very fiber of our Pentecostal experience was woven into worship. I remember the old saints testifying about being a holy roller and being saved, sanctified and baptized with the Holy Ghost and with fire. Many came out their pew clapping their hands, speaking in tongues, and dancing in the spirit. It was nothing unusual to have an old saint of God take five minutes of rejoicing during their testimony of God's delivering power. Where has our worship gone?

As a child, I remember many sermons never being finished because people stood to their feet worshiping God. It seemed more important than the third point of the sermon! Where have we missed it? One minster told me in 2014 that it had been at least five years since his church had experienced a "shout down" or had a message in tongues.

I have been concerned with the lack of spontaneous worship over the last few years in our holiness meetings. I prayed and asked God, why the drought of worship? I felt the Lord began to deal with me that the reason the people of God are having a hard time worshiping in church is because they do not worship anywhere else!

The reason the old timers had no problem worshipping at church was because they

- worshiped at home;
- worshiped in the field; and
- worshiped every spare moment they had.

Their worship was not an act; it was a lifestyle! When they came to church, worship was second nature.

This all started in Acts chapter 2 when the bystanders supposed the new "holy rollers" to be drunken men. The Church came out of the upper room full of the Holy Ghost and exalting the resurrected Christ.

In August 1801, Barton W. Stone led a revival in Cane Ridge, Kentucky, that became the most famous camp meeting. The meeting lasted a week; twenty-three thousand people attended. Often these people produced strange physical manifestations throughout the meeting. Some fainted and fell to the ground, slain in the spirit. Some exhibited uncontrollable shaking, which they called the jerks. There was dancing, running, singing—all of which Stone said were manifestations of God's presence.

In the book *They Gathered at the River*, Bernard Wiesenberger tells of the Cane Ridge revival. He said there were many manifestations of the power of God moving on people—runners, jumpers, leapers, crawlers, walkers, shouters, rollers, whirlers, dancers, prancers, shakers, bawlers, and squalors—and they were all speaking in tongues! He said, "The noise of the meeting was so great that some said, 'The noise was like the roar of Niagara.'" Where has our worship gone?

There is a downward trend we must avoid. I submit to you four steps that have been observed that lead to a shell of the "used to be."

1. **People stop worshiping**. They sit during song service. There is no hand clapping or hallelujahs. Hand raising and shouting are rare.
2. **Weak altar services** followed.
3. Shortly after, **dead services** began to be the norm.
4. The end result is a **dead church.** The youth are gone. The young couples are gone. The vision is gone, but worst of all, the Holy Ghost is gone!

There are twelve different tribes of Israel. In the Old Testament, when the children of Israel went into battle, they did not send

- Levites (ministers);
- Dan (judges);
- Issachar (scholars);
- Zebulen (businesspeople), or
- Gad (warriors).

The Lord said Judah (praise) *shall go up* first! Before we preach, He must be praised. Before we judge and bring the hammer down, He must be lifted up. Before we teach, He must be worshiped. Before we partake in business, He must be put at the pinnacle. Before we go to war with the evil of our hour, Christ must be exalted to His rightful place!

Let us get back to the worship our God deserves. We must not hold back, but turn loose and let this world know there are still people who know how to worship the Lord!

Finally, located ten miles west of Salina, Kansas, the Smoky Hill Weapons Range is the largest and busiest Air National Guard bombing range in the nation, encompassing fifty-one square miles. People were complaining about the noise of the planes. The Air Force put up a sign that read "Pardon the noise; it's the sounds of freedom!"

Well, I said I wouldn't tell it to a living soul

How He brought salvation and He made me whole.

But I found I couldn't hide such love as Jesus did impart.

Well, it makes me laugh and it make me cry.

Sets my sinful soul on fire

When God dips His love in my Heart!

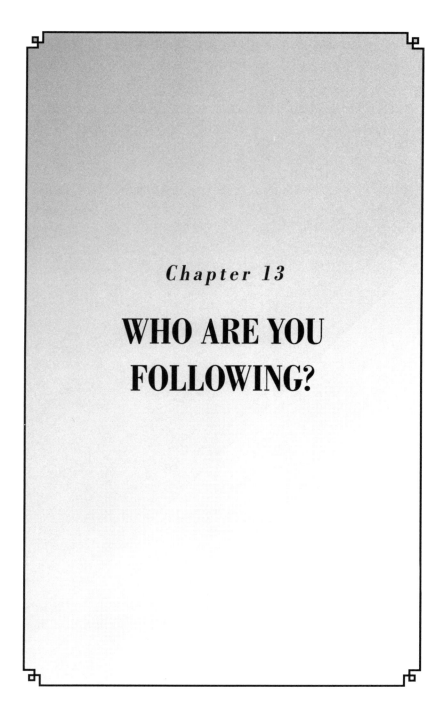

Chapter 13

WHO ARE YOU
FOLLOWING?

In our culture, the term "follow" is used to indicate how one person monitors another's activity on social media. For example, "Suzy follows Sarah on Twitter." Thirty years ago the only way you "followed" someone in this context was to have close contact with them via personal interaction, exchange of written notes or letters, or phone calls.

Allow me to offer a quote told to me by a successful businessman with a degree from a public university. He said, "I feel that someone should condemn being involved in Twitter, Facebook, or other up-and-coming social sites. As far as I am concerned, they have little or no use for anyone, much less the child of God. I hate to think that people in our church can identify with this. Before I cancelled my Facebook account a few years ago, I had already been contacted and had interaction with old girlfriends, and all manner of people that I had no business interacting with in this manner. It is a hotbed of trouble."

Public society used to call a man who followed a woman who was not his wife or family member a stalker. Now it is commonly accepted, even in the church, for married men to follow single young women, only now they call them a friend. We have married women following single young men under the auspice of being friends. Is it friend or foe?

Ethical boundaries are being ignored and obliterated.

Moral values are being thrown to the wind by insecure individuals who need to build a personal following to make them feel important. They judge their importance by how many "followers" or "likes" they accumulate.

Comments are posted about the men of God, the things of God, and the preaching of the Word of God that would never be said face-to-face. Simply because there is a screen to hide behind, they spew their negativity, proving they have replaced God with themselves upon the throne of their heart. People comment in any way they see fit because of the false anonymity they feel by being disconnected by a screen from the person or events they comment on.

So-called Christians follow Hollywood stars who oppose the very mention of the name of Christ and openly promote the sins that He shed his precious blood to remedy.

Some so-called "dedicated followers of Christ" follow secular *music icons* who spread their wicked blasphemy though the earbuds of this godless generation.

We have individuals who boast themselves as being "holy" yet follow fitness experts and justify following them because it promotes a healthy lifestyle, ignoring the fact that the promotional photos displayed are indecent and lustful.

Others are posing as "concerned Christians" who are gossipmongers following backsliders, who make a mockery of everything they once stood for, lived, and preached.

We following them?

John Piper said, "One of the great uses of Twitter and Facebook will be to prove at the Last Day that prayerlessness was not from lack of time."

Pete Cashmore, founder of the website Mashable, said, "We are living at a time when attention is the new currency: With hundreds of TV channels, billions of websites, podcast, radio shows, music downloads and social networking, our attention is more fragmented than ever."

And we wonder why there is no revival!

- Young adults, sitting in pews, pretend to use their Bible on their phone or iPad, all the while surfing the web or checking social media updates.
- Middle-aged mothers are more worried about their "bathroom mirror selfie" making them look fat than why their marriage is on the rocks.
- Teenagers post photos of themselves, lips puckered, presenting themselves in some provocative pose, at the same time claiming to be dedicated to representing Christ to this lost generation.
- Homes are in disarray.
- Husbands engage in a virtual gaming world all hours of the night while their families sleep.
- Intimacy between husbands and wives wane.

Why? All because they are consumed with their own lust in a virtual world that will leave them old, cold, empty, and alone. One preacher recently scolded a group he was talking to for "drooling over this world."

Some may entertain the thought that I have an out-of-date opinion on this issue. However, my basis for believing this way is anchored in the words of Jesus in Luke 9:23: "And he said to them all, If any man will come after me, let him deny himself, and take up his cross daily, and follow me."

We must stop following people and start following God again!